THE POWER OF LETTING GO

DISCOVERING THE REAL YOU

Cover design by Terrance Banks
Photo by Steve Nguyen

Brooks-Baldwin Publishing
P.O. Box 4462, Berkeley, CA. 94704

ISBN 978-1-976-89470-1

Special thank you to my mom, Ellen "Simply DaVene" Patton for life and giving me the best even when we didn't have much at all. This book is dedicated to you, a true artist who lived your life on your own terms. Thank you to my wife, Abigail Garcia Patton, for being my life partner and sharing the rest of this precious life journey with me. And thank you to my son, Rozcoh Luis Patton, for teaching me the greatest lesson I could ever learn. "You are my best friend in the whole world."

"The Master stays behind:

That is why she is ahead.

She is detached from all things;

That is why she is one with them.

Because she has let go of herself,

She is perfectly fulfilled."

-    Tao Te Ching

Table of Contents

Introduction

This book reflects a culmination of life altering experiences that I underwent starting when I turned twenty-eight years old and my mom came to live with me. I was living in a one-bedroom apartment and I was just beginning to really get the hang of my new life as a professional working adult with little responsibility outside of my "self" and my job. At the very same time that my mom needed to move in with me, I was in the process of breaking up with my girlfriend of six years and recording my first music album entitled "Don't Call Me John" which got published on ABB Records only months after my mom had arrived. My album dropped in the summer of 1999 and in the fall of 1999, I started my first semester as a doctoral student in the African Diaspora Doctoral program at U.C. Berkeley, with the goal of teaching classes on Hiphop Culture one day. But as soon as classes began and I started performing shows to promote my music, my mom's health spiraled and she ended up in critical condition at Highland Hospital in Oakland. Before being convinced that it was time to go to the hospital (my mom was from North Carolina and going to the hospital was always a last resort), she spent weeks and probably months in serious pain. At night I would wake up regularly from hearing her moaning in agony. Focusing on school became impossible and music became a cathartic endeavor that kept me going.

Towards the end of my second year in the doctoral program, I decided to leave the program and pursue my music career full time. I wanted to give myself the opportunity to put one hundred percent into my art and my business. I also felt that the only way that I was going to be able to really help my mom was through the type of money I could make in the music and business world. That summer in 2001, I said yes to an overseas tour to Japan and Australia as the DJ for Souls of Mischief. When we got back to the states, I simply could not return to my previous life after experiencing the type of joy and freedom I did on the road with the Souls. I felt that my mom was now healthy enough, so I put my futon mattress in the back of my truck, told my mom that I was going to Los Angeles to make some "real" money and I headed down Interstate 5 without a job nor an apartment waiting for me. Nonetheless, I felt the most alive I had ever felt in my entire life and that is when my spiritual journey that is captured in this book began.

Although I am not from Los Angeles originally, I finished high school there at Crenshaw High, Class of 1988. During those years, gangbanging and selling crack cocaine was at an all time high. I managed to survive, however, a few of my friends didn't. But one of my best friends from high school was still there in the old Leimert/Crenshaw District neighborhood, and he was one of the first people I connected with. I spent the next three years living in, and many times on, the streets of Los Angeles experiencing the beautiful *rawness* of life.

The fast pace and aggressive lifestyle of the Crenshaw District taught me a lot about trusting your instincts and intuition, how to read people and situations, how to tap into your desire to live, how to make something from nothing and to appreciate the moment because "here today, gone tomorrow". At the time though, I thought I was just learning to survive in my old neighborhood. At one point, I lost my substitute teaching position at Inglewood High because of credential paperwork that was going to take six months to process. With substitute teaching being my main income at that time, I became extremely creative (to say the least) in finding ways to survive. I was also still paying the rent at my old apartment in Oakland where my mom was staying, plus my rent in Los Angeles. So the first thing that I did was to give up my apartment in

Los Angeles and I started sleeping in my car. I remember sitting on the porch at my best friend Chayel's house and our homeboy pulled up with this huge truck that he said he got from the Salvation Army. He said that they even had RVs. Ding! That was it! I went to the Seven Eleven store and picked up one of those recycle papers where people would sell used cars and I found an RV for a little over $1000. On the outside that RV looked like an abandoned shelter, but I fixed up the interior so plush that it was like living in an Ikea furniture store exhibit. I could easily fill this whole book with story after story after story, but what is most salient about each experience, is that they led me to people, places, books and ideas that later became the themes and lessons that I decided to write about in this book.

During those three years in Los Angeles, one of the things that really forced me to re-evaluate life overall was the presence of severe nosebleeds that I began to have only months after arriving to Los Angeles. With no full time job or medical benefits, I was forced to figure out on my own why I kept having these nosebleeds, that would bleed profusely and sometimes several times a day. It was extremely scary, and at one point I was convinced that I was going to die. Although I became depressed every time my nose bled, at the same time the thought of death became very liberating for me. Once the nosebleed would stop, I would have an incredible urge to experience life to the fullest, thinking that any moment could be my last. I did things within those three years living in Los Angeles that the practical side of me would never do!

But those nosebleeds led me to develop an invaluable practice that later changed my life. I started journaling daily, recording what I ate and what I was doing every time I experienced a nosebleed. After going from clinic to clinic, the most useful information I received was that my blood pressure was high. I was barely thirty, so it was hard for me to believe that my blood pressure was causing the nosebleeds but I began documenting everything that I was eating, even the ingredients on the back of the package. One of my new friends at the time, Troy, was a model and really into fitness. He told me that most packaged foods contained a high level of sodium and that sodium caused the body to retain water and also raise blood pressure. It was like I was back in graduate school doing research. Every bit of data pertaining to the subject was extremely important and in this case the subject matter was my "life"! Little did I know at the time, that these nosebleeds that caused me so much heartache and worry, would lead to much of the impetus, knowledge and practices that I would later incorporate into my curriculum at U.C. Berkeley and my work as a life coach.

But as my time in Los Angeles became more and more turbulent and uncertain, I decided to go back to the place where life started for me as a child. Summer of 2004, I moved back to Brooklyn, New York to live with my cousin Adrienne. Both my aunt and uncle had passed away so Adrienne let me sleep in their room. Their spirits definitely came back to visit me and I felt both of them talking to me as they did when I would visit them in the summer time. In the quiet stillness of their old Brooklyn brownstone, I sat everyday and reflected; I began to piece together all the pieces of my three-year journey in Los Angeles and even parts of my journey prior. As I would sit in their bedroom window at night, I remembered how off guards my aunt and uncle's room was. But now years later, not only were they gone but also the old neighborhood was becoming gentrified. However, a thought came to my mind that gave me a feeling of peace and serenity. I had an epiphany that as things and people changed, my memory of them began changing too. What doesn't change? As I cogitated that question, my fascination with the idea of "time" and "reality" grew.

Since that summer of 2004, sitting in my aunt and uncle's room in Brooklyn, I've dedicated the remainder of my life to earnestly listening to my intuition, studying my "self"—my habits and my mindset and working to transform my reality. One of the results has been writing this book. The purpose of writing this book is merely to honor what the experiences, significant folks along the way, the books and my reflections have taught me. The thesis to my spiritual journey is: If you don't know who you are, then you don't know who you can become. Thoughts plus actions equals reality. Letting go of fear, negative thoughts created by my ego and letting go of Western notions of time (through active meditation and stillness) allowed me to access my authentic "self"--spirit. As I began to tap into my spirit (referred to in this book as either heart, gut, soul or subconscious mind) by studying my "self" and developing the relationship between my mind, body and soul, I've been able to discover the freedom I once felt as a child and generate happiness internally from an infinite source as opposed to searching for happiness through others and material things. Learning to let go has allowed me to love my "self" and in loving my "self" I've been able to now fully love others and many events/things that at first glance may seem negative but are ultimately for my greater good. Letting go has allowed me to become debt free, take risks, speak from the heart, become a husband and father, say goodbye to my mom and simply live a more purposeful and peaceful life. It is a process that never stops and is constantly evolving and changing similar to the universe itself.

Do you know what you want in life and what fulfills you? Can you distinguish between your egoic-mind and your spirit-mind? Are you able to listen to and hear your spirit-mind and do you trust what it tells you enough to follow it? Lastly, are you happy and what is your happiness contingent upon (is your happiness based heavily on outside things, people, relationships and circumstances)? Use The Power of Letting Go as a daily handbook. Start a "life journal" for yourself and begin answering these questions periodically throughout each waking day. What else are we living for if not to fully understand our "self" and our life journey? Realize your strengths and gifts. Begin to understand your purpose in life. Most importantly, discover and decide your purpose for yourself. Follow *your* heart! A purposeless life can become monotonous, exhausting and stressful. If you want, and I mean *really* want to eliminate stress and find balance and happiness that resonates from an internal source then read this book with intent, address the questions throughout the book in your journal and follow the suggestions at the end of the chapters. Transforming your life is like transforming your body. You will not get significant results until you:

1) analyze and take inventory of your diet and routine, 2) develop an image of how you want your body to look and feel, 3) create strategies and a new routine that will achieve results and 4) put forth actions daily until it becomes your new way of life and you achieve the body you want. And although this book calls on you to focus on your mind and spirit, I encourage you to include the health and maintenance of your body in order to achieve complete success.

Much Love,

Quamé

What It Means To Let Go

"Learning to let go is necessary because life is a process of continual change and transformation."

- Deepak Chopra

What does it mean to "let go"? What it means to let go can be broken down into three states of being: 1) having faith, 2) following your heart, and 3) transcending time. When you exercise and incorporate these three states of existence, you will manifest the *power of letting go*. To actualize the power of letting go, you must *let go* of three things (or states of being): 1) fear, 2) egoic thought and 3) the past and future. The rewards from exercising this power to "let go" will be *freedom*, freedom from an endless list of undesirable states of being. When you examine the term itself "let go", the term implies that something is being released or that something was being restrained. "Let" means to allow and "go" means to proceed or move. Thus, when you let go, you allow your "self" to move and be able to proceed with life. This is true freedom. Freedom is the opportunity to live, beyond merely existing physically, but to be able to *experience*. In the movie *Up In The Air*, George Clooney's character is a man who has mastered the art of letting go. At a seminar, he is giving a motivational speech around the subject and he poses the following question: "How much does your life weigh?" He then asks the audience to imagine that they are carrying a backpack and to start packing that backpack with all the stuff they have in their life. He suggests that they start with the little things from their shelves and draws and then proceed to the larger things like their clothes, television, furniture, etc. I can feel the weight just thinking about my own backpack and I live pretty modestly. Last, he asks the audience to add all of the largest items like their bed, car and home whether it's a studio apartment or a five-bedroom house. After you imagine all your "stuff" you've accumulated in life in your backpack he says, "Now try to walk." Of course, it would be impossible to walk or even move for that matter with all that stuff in your life backpack. But as George Clooney's character says, this is what we do every day, we weigh ourselves down with stuff until we can't even move. And we haven't even considered the emotional baggage from toxic relationships to stagnating jobs. Mr. Clooney's punch line to the whole backpack scenario matches the premise of this book when he says, "Moving is living." This is what the power of letting go offers a person, the freedom to live. The more you live, the more you evolve mentally, emotionally and spiritually. The world becomes larger and smaller at the same time. Ideas of what is good or bad become irrelevant. Less becomes more.

But first take inventory of your "life backpack". How much does it weigh? Imagine being offered a million dollars to live one year with only what you can keep in a backpack. You don't have to sleep on the street or anything too drastic because there are always places to stay. Could you pull it off? Most people would definitely try for a million dollars even if they had a family. What would you put in your backpack? Imagine not being responsible for tons of "stuff". I was actually faced with a similar scenario. I had moved to Los Angeles to pursue a music career and things were going pretty well for me musically. However, I could only do work that allowed me free time to work on my music with other musicians so I became a substitute teacher. I was still paying the rent for my apartment in Oakland because my mom was staying there. After a while, I couldn't afford to pay both rent in Los Angeles and Oakland. I was faced with a dilemma. My backpack was simply too heavy and I needed to take something out. I had to make a choice. One day while sitting on the porch with one of my best friends, Chayel, a friend of ours drove up in this huge truck and he told us how he got it for almost nothing from a charity organization. All of a sudden I got an idea to buy a used RV, fix it up and live in it instead of paying rent or continue living in my car, which I was doing at that time. I found an affordable RV and had a grand time fixing up the interior. It was like a miniature apartment. Friends would come by and want to hang out more in my RV than when I had my apartment. Plus, my dream of living by the beach was actualized. I found RV parks on all my favorite beaches. And I saved a ton of my money but more than that I was mobile. Funny enough, I discovered that what I feared I would need the most, electricity, served more so as a barrier between the natural sun light and me. With no electricity, I found myself waking and falling asleep to the natural rhythm of the sun. I had more energy and my moods were lighter. As well, I couldn't come home and watch television for hours and I only ate fresh foods that couldn't spoil. I lived in that RV for eight months and those were some of the most exhilarating months of my entire life, along with my freshman year in college and my summer trips home to New York. All three of those different points in my life were so enjoyable because they were all times when my life backpack was the lightest.

But what if you have family, children and responsibilities that don't allow you to simply take out heavy items like your apartment, car and the flat screen television? Well, like George Clooney's character realized toward the end of the film, life is best experienced with balance and harmony. This is why *taking inventory of your life backpack* is necessary. Sometimes, what you think you need, is absolutely not necessary and may be the thing that is making your life heavy and stagnant. For Mr. Clooney's character, his entire life fit into a carry on and he made no room for lasting relationships with family or romantic interests. Though he obtained the space and freedom to move throughout life quickly and gain different experiences, he realized toward the end of the film that the moments of stillness created from being with his family and love interest gave his life even greater meaning and a deeper sense of purpose. On the one hand, he had mastered letting go and was able to connect with people wherever he went without having to possess them. While on the other hand, his love for his job that allowed him to travel and live without a lot of stuff became a "possessive type of love" that turned into fear. He feared change and closeness, especially with his family. Thus, the key to everything we do is to find balance.

Having faith, following your heart and transcending time (not being concerned with the past or future) will give you "true" freedom to evolve spiritually while alleviating the stresses and burdens caused by too much "stuff" in your life backpack. What you choose to put in or take out your backpack is up to you. And just because you take something out to free up a little space and create lightness doesn't mean that you can't put it back in later. However you decide to pack your life backpack is up to you and can never be wrong or right, it's all about how it "feels" on your back and can you walk. Balance is essential.

JOURNAL EXERCISE:

Take inventory of your "life backpack". Write out your list of all the things you are responsible for from relationships and children to your most valuable assets. Categorize your list according to the level of stress/demand attached to each item or your need for the item. Are there items that take more energy from you than they give? What items can you absolutely not live without? How might you re-arrange, delete or add items that may bring more harmony and balance to your life. Remember that the goal is to protect your "lightness" (or happiness).

For instance, if you're a college student, you may determine that you're taking too many pre-requisite classes and maybe an elective or two will make the load feel lighter. If you're a parent or head of the household, possibly adding a certain number of days within the week reserved for things you would like to do (possibly all by yourself) creates balance. If you manage a multi-million dollar corporation, possibly spending more energy and time with family and friends will allow you to enjoy the things money can't buy. Whatever the case; write out your list, evaluate, make some decisions and then take action!

To Have the Ultimate Faith (Let Go of Fear)

"Whatever you concentrate on, you empower."

- Stuart Wilde

Having faith means that you are able to trust and believe, even in things beyond your mental conception or vision. The strongest faith may be said to rest in the belief of God (by whatever name you may choose) or a supreme force. Conceptually, God is believed to incorporate all that is and is the sum of all things. If you truly believe in God and the power of God, then you also believe in your "self" and in others as well because essentially God is a part of all that is. Ancient societies have taught that God operates through LOVE, a unifying force that serves to connect all that is. To truly understand and access love, one must let go of FEAR. Fear is a distorted perception of love that disrupts our connections in life and inhibits our thoughts, feelings and actions. Fear inhibits movement and movement represents life. Thoughts that create fear within you prevent you from being able to believe and trust in your "self", others and essentially all things in the universe.

The ultimate lack of faith is no longer believing or trusting that God is perfect and that all things happen with purpose. Subsequently, the ultimate faith is having true love for your "self", others and all other things in the universe. This love will allow you to trust and believe in your "self" and all things in the universe because all things are interconnected to form perfection or God. However, this love must be a type of love that transcends the love derived from the physical world. In order to have the ultimate faith you must exercise the ultimate love. Ultimate love is unconditional. This means that despite appearances and perceptions, you are able to understand that somehow and in some way you are connected to another individual or thing. In his book Stillness Speaks, Eckhart Tolle writes; "Feeling the oneness of you with all things is true love." The compassion and energy you are able to give yourself is usually reflective of the compassion and energy you are able to give another. When you are able to "let go", this symbolizes that you are able to believe and trust not only in others but also in your "self". You trust that others will do the "right" thing or are at least capable at some point of doing the right thing. You give them the freedom to fall or rise in any given moment. The ultimate love will allow you to see beyond concepts of "good" or "bad" because those signify conditional states.

Thus, you can trust that whatever decisions you or another person makes, are always serving a greater purpose, as God is always working on our behalf. Understanding the unity of all things, not just conceptually but through practice (ultimate love), you can realize the power to let go and as we say in church, "let god". I interpret this popular quote, "Let go and let God", to mean that when you truly believe and trust in God, you can accept and appreciate what is. But more importantly, if you understand that you are a part of God, then you can begin to trust and believe in your "self". However, this belief will hold little significance if you do not know your authentic "self". Because to know your "self" is to know your heart, and you cannot follow your heart if you do not understand what it's saying to you.

JOURNAL EXERCISE:

Write out a list of your fears. What are some of your greatest fears? How has fear prevented you from being happy in the past? How might fear be stunting your happiness currently?

Love and Fear

"The only way to master love is to practice love."

- Don Miguel Ruiz

Love is having everything but possessing nothing. Love is more than an emotion or feeling felt within one's body. Love is the magnetic force that bonds the universe and allows energy to become matter. The force of love resonates within every atom and cell throughout the entire universe and can be felt through powerful vibrations within the body. As humans we feel these vibrations and are led by them. Our objective minds interpret these vibrations as emotion. Love forms the matrix through which all other emotions are born. Fear is the weakest state of love, thus becoming love's opposite self. As love's opposite self, fear is necessary so that love may be perceived and appreciated. As with all things in the entire universe, the opposite self gives birth to the authentic self. Darkness gives birth to light, stillness gives birth to movement, woman gives birth to man and love gives birth to fear. Thus organically fear is neither negative nor positive, fear is a vibration felt within the body that gets interpreted by the mind. While fear is a product of the conscious mind, love is the essence of the subconscious mind. The subconscious mind or spirit learns about fear from and through the conscious mind. Fear arises when there is an absence of love (or a disconnection from one's true spirit). This is because as our emotional vibration level decreases, the mind interprets the sensation as a lack of connection with the world and the universe. Thus, the reaction produces emotions such as anger, jealousy, sadness, greed and revenge. These emotions that arise from the state of fear (lower vibration levels) are distorted states of love. However, when our state of mind is ruled by pure love we see our "self" in all things throughout the universe. Everything becomes simply just another version of our "self" – the universe is understood as one whole existing as fragments. The initial feeling may be referred to as falling "in love". This is because when we experience a connection to something or someone, we enter a vibrational space that is much like coming home. It may feel as if you have walked inside a place called *love*. But what you are experiencing is a connection to the moment allowing you to transcend time and tap into higher vibrations that resonate within love's energy field. This initial feeling of falling "in love" can always be felt by staying in the moment, because the moment is the only place where we can find "pure love". If love comes to you through a memory, thought or image, that love is not pure; it is simulated love created by our mind. Staying in the moment ensures that your stay inside love is not ephemeral.

Thus, through eyes of love, the universe is abundant and ideas such as death and loss become concepts that only serve to reinforce love's opposite self - fear. Faith, being the ultimate acknowledgement of God or Love (the unseen), cannot exist wherever fear is prominent. Through eyes of fear, you become afraid that you have lost something or may potentially lose something. This idea undergirds the notion that things may be finite and ruled by time. A fearful state of mind causes us to try and control circumstances and others, because we have been convinced that our connection to things/others can only be achieved through a physical connection. This is why as we become more and more attached to events and things in the physical world a sense of fear begins to eat away at our light (spirit). The mind begins to think that what the body experiences is "real". In becoming overly attached to material items and phenomena experienced in the physical world (through the five senses), we move further away from pure love or our true "self" toward the distorted end of love. It is a distorted sense of love because the greater the idea (or fear) that we may lose something, then the greater the sensation or illusion of love. It becomes like a pain that feels good. In order to maintain possession of this feeling (created by a false idea/interpretation) that we believe is love, we may try to control that which we have become attached to.

Are you the type of person that tries to control people? If you're not sure, ask yourself the following questions:

1. Do you get upset when others do not do and/or say what you expect or like from them?

2. Do you offer people advice so that they will not make "mistakes"?

3. Do you find yourself trying to understand another person's choices and/or actions?

If you answered yes to any of the three questions above, then you have tried to control someone, whether consciously or unconsciously. The issue of control relates directly to love and fear. The issue of control is an issue of power; power is a ruling force. You can generate power either through love or fear. Growing up in a gang environment, I've known many people who derived their power from fear tactics. For them, control of others was essential to maintaining their power - either through weapons, manipulating peoples' emotions or controlling what people can do in the neighborhood. Even some parents use fear tactics to control their children through punishment and chastisement. However, seeking to control is not true love because true love is unconditional. True love does not seek to control others. Thus, in order to experience true or pure love, one must be willing to let go of love's opposite self - fear. "There is nothing to fear, but fear itself."

However, when you lack balance you try to control others in fear of losing your attachment or connection. Try and imagine this idea of controlling others through the example of driving and controlling a car. When you drive a car, you are trying to arrive at a destination by controlling the vessel. This requires that you: 1) have a vehicle, 2) know how to drive, 3) have a destination in mind and 4) stay focused on your path and journey. Before you even begin your trip, you must first have faith in your own ability to drive as well as faith in others who also share the road along the way. Through faith or trust, you control the vessel with love. Once you begin driving, you cannot control how others drive (though many still try anyway and end up in road rage). You can only control your car. We are the captains of our own ship. To have the ultimate faith you must be willing to let go of fear – fear of accidents, how others drive, fatalities, not making it to the destination at a certain time and fear of the unknown or detours. If you cannot trust yourself to be able to properly control the car (our body, thoughts and emotions) then you are not ready to drive (in traffic at least). Driving implies movement and movement is life. Whenever you try to control another person, you actually lose partial and sometimes complete control of your own vessel. Constructive driving stops because you as the driver are no longer focused on your own path and are more so concerned about the driving maneuvers of another. Though it can be frustrating to watch others driving dangerously or in a way that may bring harm, the honest truth is that no matter how much you may try, you can only effectively drive your own car. However, many people do choose to abandon their own car so that they can either ride with others or help someone else drive their car. Whatever the case, your "self" journey is abandoned or put on hold. Life is put on hold and ultimately, this seemingly loving act (in seeking to help control someone else's vessel or thoughts/actions) stems more so from fear. Fear that people won't make it to their own destination; fear that nobody wants to ride with you and you may end up alone; fear that others will not do what you want them to. The ultimate act of love in this case would be to *consciously* drive your own car with complete trust and belief in your own abilities as well as the abilities of others. Even if another lacks the driving skills that you currently possess, through faith you may be understanding and compassionate in knowing that others have the ability to potentially possess these same skills and greater. And in order to protect your car from colliding with someone who has poor driving skills, simply drive your car with awareness. Our behavior and actions will inevitably influence the behavior and actions of others. To impress upon others the act of effective driving, simply be an effective driver yourself.

There's a story about Gandhi that reminds me of this idea about "self-mastery". A man once came to Gandhi after learning that sugar was detrimental to the man's health. He asked Gandhi how to go about stop eating sugar. Gandhi said come back in two weeks for the answer. In two weeks the man returned and asked Gandhi, "Why did you have me wait for two weeks to get the answer?" Gandhi replied, "Because I had to stop eating sugar." Instead of controlling others, we must first experience and be the lesson that we want others to learn. To spread love we must BE LOVE.

As the Universe in totality is connected through an invisible magnetic force, humans in totality are connected through this same magnetic force that we call love. But to experience love we must let go of fear, fear that others are incapable of making the correct choices for her/his own life path and the fear of death. Death is a human concept that symbolizes that something is lost, has ended or is finite. Death represents our attachment to the physical world. But energy cannot die, only transform. Life is infinite and humans are constantly transforming. When this transformation is viewed through a lens of loss or fear, we suffer emotionally because we believe that happiness, love and peace are not ours to experience forever. Yes, love cannot exist without faith. Faith cannot exist without both internal (spirit) and external (the outside world of the mind) awareness. Awareness cannot exist without pure consciousness (alignment of the mind, spirit and body). Pure consciousness cannot exist without focusing and being fully present in the eternal moment. Only within the eternal moment can we utilize our power of choice, our ultimate power as humans. By choosing to have faith, awareness and live fully in the moment, we choose love. By choosing love, we are able to let go of the need or desire to control others. We may provide road maps; give a person driving tips when requested, provide assistance to others in need of engine maintenance and even pull over from time to time to take a break in the journey.

But love does not require that we abandon our journey in order to control traffic.

Knowing Your "Authentic Self"

"Your life's spiritual goal consists of experiencing and stepping above whatever circumstances you find yourself in. Anything that you find difficult or arduous is almost always your main karmic challenge."

- Stuart Wilde

Have you ever heard the saying, "Nobody knows you like your mother"? My mom would tell me all the time, "I know you better than you know yourself because I carried you for over nine months." I resisted this notion that my mother could know me better than I could know my own "self", especially once I became a teenager. And the older I got, the more and more I would resist believing this statement because there were many things my mom never even witnessed or could imagine I was doing. I would think to myself that my mom may know me as the child I came to the world as but I've *changed* and there is so much about me as an adult that she just doesn't know.

It took me forty years to realize that my mom actually does know me better than I know my "self". Why? Firstly, I realized that my authentic or true "self" is my spirit not my body or even my mind. Our spirit operates through vibrations. Have you ever heard people say, "Hey this place has a nice vibe", or "I'm not feeling the new guy at work"? That language is symbolic of the fact that everything at its core is energy. In scientific terms, all matter is made up of atoms and the human body is the result of billions of atoms that have magnetically joined together to form a single object. The human brain allows us as humans to experience this physical world of countless atoms in the distinct way that we do. Thus, instead of seeing everything as actual atoms, the brain via our eyes restricts the information, only allowing us to see a larger version that we refer to as objects. Although everything is light, even sound, our brains process the information in a way that protects the human body and provides us the ability to interact and function within the Earth's environment. Our brains are like radio receivers that read frequencies that allow bits of information floating throughout the airwaves to enter us. Many of the frequencies are inaccessible. Similar to a radio, there are channels of information (radio stations) that we just can't get, but they exist, no different than how a dog and other animals can tell when a terrible storm is near or hear a whistle that resonates on an octave unrecognizable by the human brain. Thus, in scientific terms, my spirit is made up of atoms that vibrate at a certain frequency. This is why people say, "Birds of a feather flock together" or "If you want to know who you are then look at the five closet people you interact with". Atoms are magnetic and only attract like atoms. This is why ancient spiritual beliefs whether Kemetian, Vedic or indigenous, hold that as spirits we choose our parents and the conditions of our arrival into the physical world. To return to my original point, my spirit chose my mother as the vessel through which I would enter into the physical world, and she chose my spirit as well. This is one reason why she knows me best. My mother knew my spirit before birth into the physical world because who we are "never stops". We are spirits taking on physical form.

Secondly, as a baby and/or child our brains are fresh clean slates. They are sponges ready to absorb information like a new computer hard drive that has not been programmed yet. However, even without the software of information that gets uploaded from parents and people on how to speak with a formal language, how to eat using utensils, how to use a bathroom and how to walk, babies come to the world already possessing innate knowledge. They know how to do all those things already just not in the formal way accepted by society. For instance, a baby knows how to eat with his/her hands and crawl to get from one point to the next and use the bathroom (right where they're sitting!). But in order to integrate into the ways of society we are "programmed".

Nonetheless, before we are programmed, we already possess likes and dislikes and know what we are attracted or not attracted to. When I was about five years old I remember my mom asking what color I wanted my room painted. I told her orange because orange was my favorite color at the time. This attraction to orange I had was not the result of inculcation or programming, I came to the planet attracted to the color orange. I knew I liked it because it made me "feel" good and I was able to recognize the "feeling" because I was in touch with my "self". This sort of information is known by our true or authentic "self" and not our minds. My mother was able to see exactly who I was and "am" before I was programmed. She interacted with my pure spirit. It's like knowing what pure orange juice is versus orange juice made from concentrate with all the additives. There is a big difference! My mother was able to witness firsthand what I was drawn to as a baby. In fact, as a baby I knew who was a potentially "bad" person, who was "good", my favorite color, what made me happy and what made me unhappy all through my ability to "feel" vibrations and recognize the energy around me.

In the novel The Alchemist, by Paulo Coelho, the author describes this ability we are all born with as learning to read and understand "the language of the universe". He tells the story of a young boy who is able to find a "hidden treasure" through his ability to: 1) follow his childhood passion, 2) take the time to reflect, 3) have the courage (transcend fear) to make choices based on his "gut" feeling as opposed to the rational choice, 4) understand that the universe (GOD) is always conspiring to create opportunities and events that will lead you toward fulfilling your "personal legend" (destiny) and 5) live life focused on the moment, as opposed to thinking about the past or future, to ensure that you are conscious and aware of the signs that the universe is using to guide you. Through these life lessons that the boy acquires from his experiences, he is not only able to find abundance but also happiness, love and peace. And his journey started with recognizing "who he was".

As I began to grasp the power of letting go, I had to address the question, "Who I am?" I had to be able to distinguish between my authentic self and my "egoic mind". I had to develop the courage to do the things that brought me joy and peace despite the reaction or judgment from others around me. I had to become secure in my own "feelings" (not necessarily emotions). I had to learn to trust my "gut" feeling and then be able to act accordingly. This often times meant acting against the grain because what was at stake was my happiness, peace and love. Now how can a person be sure of "who they are" and "what they're feeling"? If your mom is around that may be a good place to start! Even if you don't have the best relationship with your mom, you'll be surprised how much you can learn about your "self" from talking with your mom and asking a few questions. If you don't have that luxury, then possibly the next section will offer some useful strategies.

How Do You Know Who *You* Are?

"Our lives are the sum total of the choices we have made."

- Wayne Dyer

I remember in grade school being asked, "What do you want to be when you grow up?" For the life of me I don't even remember what my answer was at the time. In fact, my answer to that question has changed several times over the years. I remember telling an uncle once that I wanted to be a baseball pitcher because at the time I enjoyed playing baseball in my backyard. In the ninth grade, my government class teacher was this big tall Black man and he made learning about The Constitution and law so fun that at that point I wanted to be a lawyer. After hearing a Dj scratch with a record for the first time growing up I knew that I wanted to be a Hiphop Dj. The list can go on and on. Some things I wanted to be have stuck with me over the years and other things were momentary. I have actually grown to believe that the question of "what do you want to be when you grow up?" is very loaded and implies that as a child you are not already "some thing". In grade school, I was actually already all those things I mentioned waiting to emerge or in progress.

The question I ask my students is not "What do you want to be?" but instead I ask, "Who are you?" Have you ever asked yourself why you do the things that you do? As a very young child it was simple, I did things either because they made me happy (and if they made others happy that would make me happy) or because my mom said so. As I got older I was introduced to idea of doing things because they were necessary (responsibilities). And once I became a teenager I learned about doing things because others were doing them. Gradually, I moved away from a place that put me in touch with my inner feelings and wants. I internalized the question asked in grade school and also interpreted the question to mean that I could only primarily be one thing in life and the success of that thing was contingent upon how much money I made from doing it or how much praise I received. But over the years, I would meet tons of people who didn't enjoy what they were doing. They felt like they were stuck in their career because they had to pay the bills or because they had to maintain the image others had of them. While in college, I made the choice to do things that allowed me the freedom to be my "self". If a class, person, job or moment didn't feel right, I learned to walk away. I kept an open mind and learned through trial and error. I realized over time that I had a passion for music, teaching and service. And when doing those things in whatever capacity I did them stopped making me happy I simply moved on. For instance, the first time that I taught special education in high school I loved it! After a few semesters of doing it, I was about to go crazy; the experience no longer brought me joy. It became an arduous task and my spirit eventually felt heavy. But my fear of not being able to find another job made me feel trapped. Eventually, I confronted my fear in order to resurrect my spirit (to raise the vibrations of my true authentic "self") and I began to work on an idea for a college course that I "wanted" to teach. The idea just came to me while standing in line at a Nas concert in Central Park and it "felt good". I put my ideas on paper and created my very first syllabus. I was so excited from the thought of following through with my idea that I decided to reach out to one of mentor professors, Dr. VèVè Clark, from my alma mater U.C. Berkeley. Whether destiny or a part of my personal legend as Paulo Coelho would say, the universe provided me with many guides, signs and opportunities. Within one semester of me confronting my unhappiness, taking a moment to re-connect with my spirit, confronting fear and then acting on my "gut" feelings, I was teaching my dream course at one of the top universities in the country. Thoughts plus belief create feelings that ignite actions, and through persistent action we create reality.

But in order to get to the point of doing something I "dreamed" of doing, I first had to connect to my authentic "self" and that meant letting go of *ideas* or *thoughts* of who I thought I was or what I thought I wanted to be "when I grew up". I had to let go of my own judgments about my self and my concerns about what others thought of me. This meant letting go of things that had taken place in the past as well as things that had not even occurred yet. Sounds simple and easy enough but it took years and years of practice to begin to really live in the moment. But when living in the moment became more and more a part of my lifestyle and way of life, I soon realized that "who I am" could only be determined by what I chose to do in the moment. In fact, the answer to "Who are you?" can only be found in the eternal moment. Yes, that means that a person is whatever they are doing in any given moment. So if you just killed a bug, in that moment you were a bug killer. If you just cooked a meal then in that moment you were a cook. If you just taught a class, then in that moment you were a teacher. Whether you are excellent or not at what you're doing is another story. And whether you can demand money for what you're doing may be questionable too. Those things would depend on one's perception and judgment but has little to do with the actual fact that actions connote one's connection to the world. So to get to the essence of who you are, first understand that you are an infinite number of things. Next, you must learn to focus on the moment and what you are feeling (not necessarily thinking) in order to connect to the vibrational field surrounding you. This will allow you to be whatever it is "you" need or want to be more fully in that moment. You will know "who you are" and when you're being your authentic "self", according to the feeling that resonates within. It is a feeling, not a thought that only you will understand. From my experience, when I am doing something that speaks to the core of my authentic self, I am filled with an inner joy, peace and sense of fulfillment. The feeling just feels right, like when I was a child and I did something that I wanted to accomplish for my "self". I didn't need outside praise, acknowledgement or any reward.

Programming The Mind

"We do not attract that which we want but that which we are."

- James Allen

The mind is divided into two spheres, the conscious and the subconscious. Dr. Joseph Murphy, author of one of my favorite books on the mind entitled <u>The Power of Your Subconscious Mind</u>, writes that the conscious mind (often referred to as the objective mind) "is your guide and director in your contact with your environment. You gain knowledge through the five senses. Your objective mind learns through observation, experience and education." It is through our conscious mind that we derive our ability to *reason*. Thus, the ultimate power within our conscious mind is the power of choice. The choices you make produce your reality and essentially determine your life. When a person is convinced that they do not have a choice in a matter, they have relinquished one of their greatest powers as a human. This is why the knowledge and information you receive is vital because the choices you make are contingent upon what you know and what you don't know.

Awareness is the key to making productive and positive choices that assist our soul's evolution. This is why having awareness and knowledge is referred to as "coming into the light". The "light" is energy or essentially everything. The "light" is love while "being in the dark" represents not knowing. Usually, when one knows very little, little to no movement occurs. No movement or stasis is symbolic of fear. It's like a child that is afraid or forbidden to leave their neighborhood and knows nothing about the world beyond the radius of their community. Without the ability to experience other aspects of the world and life through the five senses, that child will be denied the ability to learn from their own experience and will have to depend on others and outside sources for information. This reminds me of the many students I've taught in inner city areas who have never had the opportunity to leave their city let alone the country. What they know about the world is supplied by media sources or someone else's experience. After getting a dose of one too many negative stories about the world, many of my students have lost their desire to leave their neighborhood. They become complacent and their ability to imagine begins to fade. Once your ability to imagine fades, so do your dreams and your motivation to chase after your dreams. One of my favorite music producers, RZA from the Wu Tang Clan, shared in an interview how he would often times skip school and go to Times Square in New York City to watch the classic Kung Fu movies of the 1980's. Also coming from an inner city environment, he found that school didn't necessarily challenge him nor feed his imagination. However, these Kung Fu films exposed RZA to new ways of thinking, living, acting and spiritual outlooks from the other side of the world that supplied him a knowledge base that increased his decision making ability. He was then able to create a path for him to do what he loved and empower others, like myself, along the way. Even if we are unable to leave our immediate environments physically, we must use our imagination to transport our spirits to different places in the universe. The information and images our objective minds are exposed to determines the choices, decisions and actions we are able to make stemming from either love or fear.

But the second sphere of the mind, the subconscious, has access to infinite knowledge and intelligence. When one has the ability to tap the powers of the subconscious mind, they will gain an awareness that is unlimited and anything once perceived as impossible by the conscious (rational) mind will become possible. Dr. Joseph Murphy writes:

> Your subconscious mind is often referred to as your subjective mind. Your subjective

mind is aware of its environment, but not only by means of the physical senses. Your subjective mind perceives by intuition. It is the seat of your emotions and the storehouse of memory. Your subjective mind performs its highest functions when your objective senses are not functioning. In other words, it is that intelligence that makes itself known when the objective mind is suspended or in a sleepy, drowsy state.

If you envision the mind as a well filled with information, the conscious mind would be at the very top of the well and the subconscious would represent the depths of the well. It is in the depths of this well that the soul resides. As Murphy states, "Your subjective mind can leave your body, travel to distant lands and bring back information that is often of the most exact and truthful character. Through your subjective mind you can read the thoughts of others, read the contents of sealed envelopes, or intuit the information on a computer disk without using a disk drive." As information is constantly entering the well of our spirit, no different than the way water might, what is mostly used is the water at the top of the well or in this case the information at the forefront of our conscious mind. However, in the depths of our subconscious mind, is an abundance of information connecting to a central source referred to as the Universe or God. And just like the water in a well, the information at the top of our minds will be either "dirty" (destructive) or "clean" (constructive) depending on the source of water. Because even though all water at its base is pure, other elements may contaminate the water and eventually harm the drinker. Our thoughts (information) form the water that fills our well. Fragments that enter through the opening at the top of the well may seep down into the depths of the well and eventually begin to contaminate a person's water supply. For as Murphy writes, "Everything has happened to you because of the thoughts impressed on your subconscious mind through belief."

Just as the subconscious mind keeps your heart beating and internal organs functioning without any assistance from the conscious mind, it is also operating to create the conditions and experiences that correspond to the thoughts in your conscious mind. The workings of the subconscious mind are involuntary and most times overlooked or taken for granted. I myself never contemplated how there is an aspect of my mind that never stops working even when I'm asleep. Even if I chose to hold my breath, at some point my subconscious would over ride my conscious decision and tell my body to continue to breathe. However, at the same time if I focused hard enough and concentrated on not breathing at all, I could create emotions through my thoughts that could eventually stop my heart from beating. While the conscious mind possesses the power of choice, the subconscious mind possesses the power of creation. The subconscious creates "feelings" while the conscious mind creates "thoughts". Feelings are vibrations that formulate the Universal language because everything at its essence is energy or atoms (which are constantly vibrating). In this regard, all feelings and emotions (energy in motion) are true. Feelings are part of nature's law and can never be false. What a person feels is always the truth. Reality is formed in the subconscious mind. However, the feelings created by the subconscious mind are subject to the thoughts created by the conscious mind. The subconscious does not reason like the conscious mind and merely reacts to the thoughts produced by the conscious mind. While all feelings are true and real, all thoughts are not. Feelings are consistent and thoughts are not. For instance, love always feels like love but the thought that created the feeling of love on one occasion may produce another emotion on another. For example, there was a time when I loved white chocolate. Every time I thought about white chocolate I would get happy and feel the internal sensation created by the emotion I felt toward white chocolate. I loved white chocolate so much that one day I bought a huge chunk of white chocolate that was over a pound. I ate a piece of it every day until I got extremely sick. The suffering I experienced left such a lasting memory that manifested itself physically. For weeks and months after getting sick, whenever I smelt or sometimes saw white chocolate, I would get nauseous. I believed that if I ate white chocolate again I would get sick. No longer did I love white chocolate. But only my perception and belief of white chocolate changed. White chocolate itself did not make me nauseous or sick, it was the belief that resonated in my subconscious. The only thing separating "me" (my subconscious or spirit) from loving white chocolate was the *belief* that I would get sick again or that I wouldn't like the taste. When the conscious mind is convinced or agrees that something is real or true, the subconscious mind creates feelings that undergird the belief. Then those feelings lead to energy or actions that manifest the beliefs. Even when your conscious mind is no longer thinking the thought, once the belief has been imprinted onto the subconscious, the subconscious then silently works to bring to fruition your beliefs similar to the way a thought can make your heart speed up or slow down without you consciously thinking about your heart. This is the power within the relationship between the conscious and subconscious mind.

The mind (brain) operates very much like a computer hard drive. Essential to the mind's ability to function and perform commands is memory. Just like a computer hard drive, your mind's performance is contingent on the amount of information stored within it. The brain calls on information stored in the memory banks within your conscious and subconscious mind. Like in the movie The Matrix, if you want to be able to do Karate, shoot automatic weapons or fly a helicopter, all you have to do is upload the information. However, unlike The Matrix, we must upload information through a learning process. This learning process can be like programming the mind where "how to" instructions and details are inputted and then the information is carried out by the body. In order for the learning process to be affective, the mind uses repetition. Repetition allows information to be more accessible. As well, repetition brings about belief and belief brings possibility and actuality.

But a computer pales to the capacity and potential power of the mind. If you do not install a check and balances program, the mind will soon power over the body and the spirit. When this occurs our soul power is limited. In The Matrix, the character Morpheus believed that Neo was capable of unlimited powers. This is why Morpheus kept telling Neo to "free his [conscious] mind" so that he could tap into his subconscious and gain access to infinite abilities. He was referring to letting go of rational thoughts produced in the conscious sphere of the mind that may be more illusion than truth. If we spend more time developing our (rational) mind without also developing our body and spirit, the mind will become over active in daily matters. Our intuitive abilities relayed by the subconscious mind will decrease if too much focus is placed on critical analysis, reasoning and rationality. This leaves little room for serendipity and spontaneous miracles. It also leaves little room to be a human animal and god-like. Can you imagine animals rising up, forming a militia and attacking the world to control land and resources? No, because the mind of non-human animals does not allow them to over think their instincts and intuition. They live in complete harmony and balance between their mind, spirit and body.

However the power of the human objective mind can be so intense that when the human ego goes unchecked or undisciplined, the result is always pain, suffering, disaster, and misery. This is because the *ego* is an aspect of the objective mind that perceives "self" as separate from the rest of the world. This aspect of our being is important however because it allows us to focus on our individual life journey and cater to our individual needs so that we may complete our spiritual mission. The ego's primary concern is the individual's interest rather than society. This is why maintaining balance between the ego and spirit is crucial so that we do not become so self-centered that we forget that our individual missions are ultimately to better the world as a whole. Thus, the result of not having a checks and balance program leads to choices that stem from a fear of loss and eventually selfishness. Throughout history this virus of fear and selfishness has led to wars, colonization, holocaust and the displacement of animals and people throughout the planet. Take a minute and reflect. What pain has your ego caused in the past?

But also like a computer hard drive, the mind cannot program itself. Who is in *control* of your mind? Who is *programming* your mind? The information itself that enters your mind or brain is important. For instance, have you ever witnessed a lot of violence for a long period of time whether it was on a television, a movie or just happening around you? Have you ever experienced being in a violent argument for a long period of time? The information taken in by the brain affects your subconscious mind and body. You will become more tense, high strung or anxious. Your spirit's vibrations will increase or decrease to match whatever it encounters. This is why your heart rate speeds up during a violent argument with lots of yelling and screaming going on. Although your vibrations may be increasing (which sounds like a good thing), the vibrations are frantic and disruptive. This is why for most people arguing does not "feel" good. It leaves the spirit and body feeling exhausted and depleted. You have exerted energy during the process to defend yourself, leaving no room to receive energy. And when we feel the need to defend ourselves, this is proof that our egos are in control, not our spirits. Some people however become accustomed to the feeling created by arguing. In an attempt to raise their energy level, they seek to argue, even though the increase of vibrations through arguing is not a healthy process. But their objective minds have convinced them that this is the only way for them to get energy, by taking it from others. This is one of the worst habits your mind can create. Similar to doing drugs or eating a bunch of sugar, you experience a quick "high" (from the increase of atoms vibrating) but the low is always lower than where you were originally resonating. Just observe a person that starts an argument. First they become defensive, get all riled up and at some point start yelling. Then when the smoke settles, they usually are extremely remorseful or become depressed. But you can choose to program your mind not to argue or start arguments. You can choose to not be a witness to violence for long periods of time, even if you have convinced your "self" that you have no choice (that's just a result of fear). When you are ready to develop and nourish your spirit so that it can evolve and grow, you will begin to monitor what enters your mind. Even when you do witness violence you will choose not to hold on to it in your memory banks, you will push "delete".

When you're ready to begin programming your mind instead of letting others program your mind for you, you will value your choices and also realize that you always have a choice in any given situation. This desire to take control of the programming process will be significant of your love for your "self", the part of you that is connected to all things. Because remember, your "authentic self" is merely a part of ALL that exists. Love is the energy that binds and connects all things in the universe. So to get energy you will choose not to rob others of their energy through arguments. Instead, you may choose to exercise or find constructive ways to increase your spirit's vibrations and release love (energy) in exchange. For the saying goes, "It is better to give than to receive". In the end, your "high" lasts longer and over time it can become permanent. This process is how our souls are shaped. Think about how you feel after working out or laughing for long periods of time. You want to continue to do things. You feel vibrant and alive. You are also more likely to want to interact and hang out with other people. And your body really loves these types of activities because it allows your body to release natural endorphins that fight pain and stress, allowing both your spirit and body to relax and enjoy life.

The conscious act of programming your mind to "love" should be one's primary objective. Why? Because there is only one emotion and everyone as a baby is born knowing only that one emotion - love. From love all the other emotions derive. The other perceived emotions like anger, sadness, jealousy, envy and fear are only degrees to which one is not experiencing love. Babies only know love. A baby crying when she/he is hungry is only representative of the fact that the baby is not getting something they need – love in the form of nourishment. Self-preservation is the first law of nature. Self-preservation is the soul's desire to live and experience the world through our senses. This is love in its most raw form. It is the highest vibration in the universe. Both the law of self-preservation and love are not concerned with rationality and tend to operate in the realm of irrationality as perceived by the objective mind. But as babies, our objective mind is not developed. We must rely on our subconscious mind that comes to the Earth already developed in order that the body may even operate and continue to develop. Without clear vision, developed muscles or the ability to speak and reason, a baby possesses knowledge in the form of feelings and emotions. Until the objective mind is developed and learns that which society uploads into her/his hard drive, a baby interacts with the world through what is in her/his subconscious mind. Thus, a baby's spirit can be looked upon as pure because her/his spirit has yet to be influenced by *thought*.

JOURNAL EXERCISE:

Programs are repeated information. In other words, programs are habits. Think about the ways you were possibly programmed as a child. What habits did you develop as a child and do you continue to perform those habits today? How have those habits served you over time? What purpose did those habits undergird? What programs or habits would you like to add and why?

Feeding Your Spirit (Godfood)

"You have to do what excites you!"

- DaVene

One morning I was talking to a colleague and friend of mine. We were discussing food and eating right. I'm always conscious about what I eat because, around the age of thirty, I discovered that I was developing high blood pressure (hypertension). Whenever my pressure would get too high I would get these nosebleeds that were very alarming and over time I thought that I was going to die. The experience made me more conscious about life. As I was telling my friend about the breakfast I had that morning, he asked me, "What did you feed your spirit this morning?" Wow! He got me with that one. I was absolutely stumped for a few seconds because although I think of myself as being enlightened, I didn't have an answer. In fact, at that moment, I couldn't recall ever having pondered the notion of "feeding my spirit". Then suddenly I remembered that I had not too long ago created a music album entitled <u>Godfood: The Break-fast</u>. The concept behind the album was that in order to create music that would nourish my soul, I would first have to abstain from fast food, television and negative elements. I chose to listen to mainly classic Soul and R&B love songs that I ended up sampling to make new compositions. The goal was to cleanse myself and then create an album that reflected my new state of mind and being. I named the album Godfood because I believed that everything I ingested for that period of time was nourishing the "god" in me. As well, the end product itself would be "godfood" in the form of music that could be a source of motivation and spiritual upliftment for the listener. Though I created a whole album based on this concept of nourishing the "god" in us, I had not kept the idea in the forefront of my consciousness. But as my memory returned, I finally offered my friend an answer. I told him that I had taken a moment to listen to the birds singing outside my window before getting out of bed to come into work. I spent the rest of the day thinking and reflecting on the different ways I feed my spirit.

How do you feed your spirit and what has your diet consisted of lately? The same way that I keep track of my meal plan so that I can keep my blood pressure down, I have gradually begun to develop my spiritual meal plan. Feeding my spirit is now a conscious act for me daily. As with all things, balance is good. With food, every once in a while I throw in something sweet or some french-fries when the craving comes from within and not from watching a commercial. Learning how to feed my spirit has allowed me to get to know my "self" even better. I'm learning what things my spirit absolutely needs, what it desires and what it doesn't like or want at all. The things that bring me happiness and peace without harming or interfering with others' lives are most necessary in my meal plan. I have learned that arguing, clutter/filth and monotonous routines bring my spirit *down* significantly. Road trips through the countryside, chilling on the beach, working out with friends, assisting someone in need, sitting in silence and sharing a hardy laugh bring my spirit up. I consciously now indulge in these activities with the objective of nourishing my spirit to keep it healthy and vibrant.

I've also come to realize that programming the mind is the same as feeding the spirit. As the mind and spirit (conscious and subconscious) share a similar space, they lead into one another. What enters your conscious mind will also visit your subconscious and whatever is resonating in your subconscious will then create your conscious state of mind. In other words, the information you program your conscious with will go down the well of your mind into your soul. "You are what you eat." Once your soul begins to digest the information, the affects will manifest themselves in the conditions, circumstances and people you find yourself surrounded by. If you indulge in gossip, you will find yourself surrounded by judgmental people or being judged yourself. If you are always listening to violent music or watching violent movies, you will find a fair amount of violence in your life. No different than the guy from the documentary, "Supersize Me", who ate McDonald's fast food every day for a month to prove a point. His unbalanced acidic diet consisting of mainly starch, refined sugar, meat and salt began to manifest in his body as illness and in his emotional state as moodiness and depression.

To nourish the spirit, one must become an active learner, an active listener and an active being. This means that a person must be engaged and totally present (fully conscious both mind and spirit) while interacting with the *foods of life*. Because what you ingest from others becomes stool that returns to the earth and fertilizes the food that the rest of the planet will eat. All things are interconnected and intertwined. But to realize one's connection, a person must first be willing to let go of the things that serve to disrupt harmony. Can you remember the last time you were able to enjoy the company of others while suffering from a stomachache, toothache or heartburn? It's impossible. Similarly, it is impossible to enjoy ourselves when our spirit is suffering from anger, jealousy and sadness. This is the result when we lack having a balanced spirit meal plan.

JOURNAL EXERCISE:

Is your spirit feeling out of shape? How do you feed your spirit? What makes you excited? And how often do you engage in the things that excite you? Create your Spirit Meal Plan. If you are a person who absolutely needs structure, use a calendar to plot out daily activities that feed your spirit (excite you or raise your energy vibrations) to ensure that your spirit is properly nourished. But don't hesitate to break from your plan and do things in the moment. After a while, feeding your spirit should become a natural part of your life. And keep in mind that not everything that feeds your spirit, you will find enjoyable initially. Some spiritual nourishment may not seem enjoyable at first, like cleaning, charity work, and rigorous exercise, but trust me you will feel the benefits afterwards.

To Follow Your Heart (Let Go of Egoic Thought)

"When you live through the ego, you always reduce the present moment to a means to an end. You live for the future, and when you achieve your goals, they don't satisfy you, at least not for long."

- Eckhart Tolle

The world may be seen or experienced through two main realities. The first reality is what I consider *pure reality*. This is the world we experience without our rational mind and even our senses. In this way, the world is simply pure matter or essentially "energy", known in the scientific community as atoms. Can you imagine what life would be like if your body felt no pain, or if you could see things as atoms, or if laws of nature like gravity didn't affect you? Sounds like Superman and Wonder Woman right? Indeed, we would be "superheroes". In fact, the idea of escaping the human condition is not new. The idea and even practices date back as far as we can trace, starting with the earliest civilizations in Africa. From medicine men to the building of the Pyramids, we have sought to transcend the limits projected by the human mind. But for the average everyday working person in modern societies like the United States, we are more concerned with secular matters like paying bills, supplying our family's material needs and making money. Spiritual matters take a back seat. Many of us lead fast paced lives that go nowhere quick. We live in an information age where instead of going to the library, asking an elder for wisdom or turning inward for answers, we refer to the Internet and television. And of course, television and computers are not bad nor are any of the modern technological inventions. Unfortunately, we have chosen to praise the speed of life (that feed our egos) offered by computers and machines over the human "magic" and richness of life offered by patience, prayer, family traditions and being one with nature. Through direct interaction with others, our "authentic self" and the natural world, we are closer to experiencing pure reality.

Funny, I remember growing up as a sci-fi buff and watching Star Trek. The idea of teleporting and riding through different space dimensions seemed to me as about as "unreal" as you can get in the early 1980's. And I loved the little flip phones they would talk to each other through. Their spacecraft actually had a huge screen that would allow you to see the person you were talking to on the other end. Keep in mind that in the early 1980's, the average person had to get home quick if they were expecting a phone call because answering machines and pagers weren't even available yet. But now in 2010, my flip phone is considered a dinosaur by my students who walk around with phones that are more advanced than the stuff in Star Trek. What we are able to imagine can become reality. Our hearts are the link between imagination and reality. When we transcend rational thought and access our imagination, we are capable of becoming superheroes.

It's pretty incredible how reality has changed within my short lifetime. But even with advances in technology that make Star Trek seem plain, the majority of people in the United States are consumers and not producers of these advances. From my observations, most of us living in the cities don't even know how to grow our own food, make our own clothes or shoes, and even make our own decisions. Far from being superheroes, as consumers we ignore what large corporations are doing to the planet so that they can profit from our insatiable appetites for material things driven by a culture of greed and individualism. What we are feeding is our "ego". And the ego never gets enough. What is to become of our planet and the natural world that is being devoured by this human monster? We have become so addicted to this fast pace of consumption, that even though most of us realize the detriment of our ways, we feel powerless to correct it or even change ourselves.

Like I said before, most of us are far from being superheroes because we see and experience the world through the second type of reality – *conceptual reality*. This reality is formed through shared mental projections, interpretations and beliefs about the world. It is made up of individual conceptual realities from every human being on the planet. In different regions and areas those individual realities are more closely connected forming pockets of shared realities called families, communities, networks, institutions and societies. As people interpret the things they see and experience based on their own thoughts, those same thoughts have been produced or affected by someone else's thoughts. This foundation of knowledge like a computer software program is inputted into each one of us as babies and children. As information like language, communication and ideas about morals, spirituality and life are uploaded, they form the filter through which we may interpret the world outside of us. Thus, in this reality, we experience the world not as it is but as our minds or the "collective consciousness filter" has already interpreted it. So immediately when we see the red ball in the sky our mind confirms that it is the sun (in English) and depending on our program, other information may register. But this is merely information and not necessarily pure reality. This shared reality does allow us to connect and share a means through which we can see and experience the world similarly, but many of us have come to believe that these "norms" created by the collective consciousness filter is the ultimate reality. Many of us are ruled by our minds and have lost touch with our own internal program that was uploaded into us before we were born. We all come to the world with knowledge and information already inside us that is communicated through "feelings" (beyond what you may consider to be emotions) or what I like to call vibrations. If we disconnect from our minds, which are no more than computer programs designed by countless other individual minds/programs, we will be able to experience the "real" as Morpheus in "The Matrix" would contend. This is because the thoughts that we believe are our own are actually nothing more than a computer program. Pure reality lies beyond what the eyes and mind encounter. You can experience the essence of something once your interaction is free of interpretation, judgment, labeling and identification. The "real" experience is felt internally, not conceived. Original thought is possible as well as connecting to ancient wisdom through some form of meditation or disconnecting from your thinking mind. Pure reality is experienced when we connect to our subconscious mind – the intuitive part of our being that is our authentic self.

This is how we can become more like super heroes, by controlling how we use our minds/egos.

So stop thinking and start feeling. If you woke up and felt something that prompts you to go to a certain location, then take a chance and go. You may experience something life changing or you may subtly acquire something at that location that later links you to a life changing experience. If you walk into a room and suddenly feel a vibration that says this place is not safe even before your mind can identify why or confirm, go with your gut and leave.

At one point I was really into playing the lottery. Each day I would sit and let numbers come to my head but I was actually thinking up the numbers instead of feeling them. One day I went to a local Seven Eleven and played some numbers I had thought up and then out of nowhere I had a feeling to fill out a sheet by simply letting my hands land on whatever numbers they chose. I believe that parts of our body can tap into an infinite source of information. Anyway, at the end of the week I forgot to look my numbers up because I hadn't been winning anything so I called my brother Troy and asked him to read the winning numbers to me. As he started reading the numbers, it was weird because on one of the sheets I noticed that the numbers were aligned with what he was saying one right after the other. In fact, the very first three numbers in a row were right! And yes you guessed it, that was the sheet where I let my hand choose and not my mind. The crazy part is, after I reflected back to how I felt when I was selecting the numbers, the first three choices came with ease. As I neared the last two numbers plus the mega number, my mind had started to intervene. The mind can be a hard beast to contain! Though I only won $7 for the three numbers, I felt like I had experienced a miracle. Needless to say, I haven't won since because my mind is active more than ever whenever I even think about playing the lottery.

Without doubt, our hearts are never wrong. Connecting and listening to your heart is the only way to access pure reality where peace, harmony and love reside. Are you able to connect and listen to your heart? Do you trust what your heart tells you or are you always second guessing your "self"? Are you a person who thinks a lot and is always weighing options and making decisions in your head? And are the activities that you use to disengage from excessive thinking healthy?

Stop Planning Your Life and Just Live It

"The whole function of money is not to *have* it; its function is to use it. The main reason for generating money is to buy experiences."

- Stuart Wilde

There are some things in life that just can't be planned. But in capitalist American culture, "planning" is very much the norm because our society is based on time and "time is money". And since money reigns supreme over God and most spiritual matters in popular mainstream American culture, the focus of our lives soon becomes driven by money and essentially matters of time. We begin to plan even the most spiritual events unknowingly. Evidence of this excessive level of planning can be found in common everyday questions we ask each other. For instance, like asking your friend who is still single (or even in a relationship too), "When do you see yourself getting married and having kids?" I wonder can you really put a date on that sort of thing? And my favorite question that is asked religiously around holidays is, "So what are you doing for Christmas (or Thanksgiving or Memorial Day or even the weekend)?" Sometimes I wonder when people are going to start asking, "Hey, when do you plan to die?" How is a person who lives in the "now" supposed to answer these questions? Easy, most of us aren't living in the "now". In order to answer these types of questions a person must shift their state of consciousness from that exact moment to a nonexistent place somewhere in their mind and "dream up" an answer. Nonetheless, these questions are indicative of living life on the clock.

As we find ourselves answering these questions, we are creating expectations and beliefs for ourselves that we later use to judge and critique ourselves by. Once I answer the question about when I plan to get married or have kids, I have created a marker, that should I miss this marker, I could become very upset or dissatisfied with my life. In our society, ruled by the clock and calendar, if you haven't done things by a certain point, you're viewed as a failure or abnormal. Think about the way we regard the older person returning to finish her/his degree or the woman in her thirties who hasn't had a child yet or the forty something year old single guy still living in a studio or with his parent(s). And how we look at these people, even in the subtlest way, is the way in which we look at ourselves. So if your marriage fails, or you don't graduate in four years or even attend college, or you simply don't have any "plans" for the future (especially Christmas or the weekend), you begin to look at yourself "differently". You begin to judge yourself as being less successful than others.

Plans do serve a purpose because when you think about it, plans take place within a moment of "pure time". Pure time means the exact moment, not the past nor future. So at one point in time, the thought or plan probably came from a sincere intention but after that moment we should be willing to let go of that original thought/plan so that a greater force or plan may happen. When we lock so firmly into our plans creating tunnel vision, we are no longer able to recognize greater events happening around us leading to a greater destination. For instance, once I had planned a trip to Los Angeles to see friends and my brother Troy who lives a few miles outside the city. It was Christmas and I planned on treating myself to a new pair of sneakers because I hadn't bought any in a while. My plan was to get some sneakers from one of the many fancy shops in L.A. and I gave myself a budget of about one hundred and fifty dollars (I really wanted some Jordans!). Anyway, I went with my "gut instinct" to take Interstate 101 instead of Interstate 5 even though Interstate 101 takes at least an hour longer. But despite my anxiousness to get to L.A., I stayed relaxed and connected to the moment knowing that I would get to L.A. right when I needed and that there was no need to hurry. That entire drive, I kept a peaceful state of mind and I drove the speed limit of 65 mph. It was incredible! I noticed the trees, the animals, the water; I noticed everything my eyes could take in. As my mind was so open from being at peace and one with the drive, I noticed just how incredibly beautiful this small area was called "Pismo Beach". I decided to actually pull over and use this spot to gas up. Usually, getting gas only takes five minutes for me, but I was so content that I enjoyed looking at all the surroundings while I was pumping gas. I noticed that there was a string of clothing outlets right across from the gas station. I had come this way before and seen these outlets but at this particular moment they stood out for some reason. I found myself staring at a huge sign that read, The Nike Factory Outlet. From my past experience, these outlets never had anything good so I didn't know why I felt the urge to go check this store out, but I went with the flow of what I was feeling and went in. Oh my God! They had a sale that was unbelievable! I ended up buying my brother three pair of Nike sneakers (real fancy too!), a warm-up jacket and a t-shirt! And I got myself two pair of sneakers and one pair was those Jordans I wanted, a warm-up jacket and a couple t-shirts all for under $150 dollars! Once I got in my car I sat for a moment to contain my excitement and I realized that had I not been so present in the moment, relieved of time constraints and willing to follow my gut, I would have totally missed this golden treasure. I had my mind set on buying a new pair of sneakers in L.A. and fortunately for me I wasn't married to the thought/plan. But my intention was sincere and it seemed that the universe worked with me in getting those Jordans as long as I was willing to deviate from my original plan.

Planning didn't become a major part of my life until after college. Before college, my plan was simple, finish high school, go to college and on to graduate school, get married, buy a house, have children and then live happily ever after. Simple right? Sounds like the American Dream but that's what I had in mind. Not sure where it came from either because that wasn't exactly the life or household I grew up in. And though that was the big picture I had in mind since I was probably around fourteen, my life before fourteen as a child was day by day. I lived in the moment and aside from maybe planning a summer trip, life was filled with spontaneity, freestyle and serendipity. Everyday after school I wasn't sure what I'd be doing but I looked forward to maybe hooking up with my crew of friends. We'd meet somewhere and ask the classic question, "What y'all feel like doing?" At that time I didn't realize the spiritual freedom involved in that simple process. We simply allowed our "selves" the space to explore our inner desires and honor our internal voices that would soon get drowned out by the voices in our heads saying, "How are you going to pay the rent?" As children, if we felt like hitch hiking to the Mall or making a tree house or acting like Kung Fu fighters or skipping school or drawing pictures or playing basketball or just doing nothing, we simply did it! However, many of my friends had a lot of responsibilities at an early age, and they didn't have ample freedom to explore their feelings. I was fortunate to have a mom that let me have plenty of time to enjoy my childhood. I didn't have as many chores or responsibilities as my other friends and when I did have to do chores, I remember doing them with a real big attitude.

Nonetheless, the freedom my mom gave me to explore and tap into "me" led to my keen "feeling antenna". By the time I turned eighteen and was entering college at U.C. Berkeley, I had a fairly developed sense of awareness, presence and ability to "read" the energy vibrations wherever I was. Though my plan was to major in Political Science, graduate and go to Law School and become a lawyer, I wasn't happy in my Political Science courses. Very quickly the thought of becoming a lawyer didn't seem so desirable either. My spirit got so low that during my sophomore year I had contemplated dropping out of school but after talking with a couple of friends at the time (thanks Damaari and Joseph!), I decided to stay in school and change my major to what I enjoyed most, African American Studies. The thought alone brought me pure joy and excitement about school all over again. The African American Studies Department taught me about "life" and answered questions I didn't even realize I had. The courses and enlightened professors fed my soul! Once I declared the major, my happiness returned completely. It was a watershed moment in my life and I didn't realize at the time the power of my decision. I was learning to follow my heart instead of my *plan.* As I reflect back to that moment and major decision I made, I realize now that having a plan is good because it is useful in producing constructive action and movement in life, but also being able to fluctuate and adjust your plan within any given moment is equally as important. Because just as your plan may help you get moving on things in life, that same plan can prevent you from reaching your greater objectives and goals. The key is to always maintain balance and stay present within the moment so that you can see the detour and warning signs that may pop up during your journey.

By my senior year of college, I wasn't sure what I wanted to do with my life. I knew I had fallen in love with all my professors and I wanted to be like them and have the same impact on others that they had on me. The Universe seemed to be on my side as an opportunity for graduate school in education and a teaching position at the local high school both opened up for me. I continued to freestyle life for the next couple of years after graduation until I landed a full time position as the undergraduate advisor in my former department back at U.C. Berkeley. I spent the next four years as an academic advisor living a very routine and comfortable life in Berkeley, except for every summer when I would go home to New York to spend a few months with my family. Funny, it was during the summer that I felt like I actually "lived" because I did things that involved more risk. Though I was happy with work, I didn't feel fulfilled because my spirit wasn't being challenged and soon my spirit began to "feel" heavy and tired. I knew that I needed a change and some movement in my life but I didn't know what my next move could be. Once again, getting silent and still allowed me to recognize an opportunity to apply to the graduate program that had just started in the department I was advising for. Upon entering the doctoral program, I figured my life was on track with my overall plan I mentioned earlier. I was on track to finish my Ph.D. by thirty-two, get married by thirty and possibly start having children by thirty-three. Funny thing is that I never once sat and questioned if any of those things were really what I wanted or where I got those ideas. By the end of my first year in the doctoral program, my mother became very ill and needed my care, I broke up with my girlfriend of six years, I wasn't enjoying my experience in the doctoral program and I released a record for fun with my friends and it actually became an underground hit! Right at thirty years of age as I was set on my path to complete all the major items on my *Life Plan Checklist*, everything went topsy-turvy. As I faced another watershed point within my life, I resisted those things that went counter to my *Life Plan Checklist* like breaking up with my girlfriend, not enjoying school and taking care of my mom. And in accordance with natural law, that which I resisted only brought more suffering. To end my depression and suffering, I decided to let go of my strict and inflexible relationship with my plans. Slowly but surely as the years passed I came to recognize and understand how the Universe was manifesting my ultimate goals and even things beyond my imagination at the time.

At this point in my life now as I write this book (in 2010), I do a very limited amount of planning, mostly that which is required in my work as an educator at the University of California, Berkeley. However, my life outside of teaching is very spontaneous, exciting and mysterious. I have grown to not only appreciate "the unknown" but now it "feeds" my soul. I even recently completed an album, with a great friend of mine (Deqawn), entitled "Talkin' All That Jazz". The album came as a total surprise to both of us. The project itself was nowhere on our radar, but in the instant the idea and possibility became present, we jumped on it and completed the album in three weeks! We had so much fun in the studio cracking jokes and telling stories; it was one of those priceless points in our lives that we will never forget or be the same after.

How often do you engage in spontaneous activities or projects that could be potentially life changing? How content are you with your life right now? Is there a balance between the "risk" factors and "stability" factors in your life? And how much of your life is a race against time?

JOURNAL EXERCISE:

It's simple – "Plan not to plan." Set time aside throughout the day, week or year where you simply "go with the flow" and allow serendipitous moments to guide you.

Feeling vs. Thinking

"Listen to your heart. It knows all things, because it came from the Soul of the World, and it will one day return there."

- Paulo Coelho

Planning involves a thought process that may disconnect you from what is happening in the present moment. Planning entails that you think about, *imagine* and envision the future. Of course, there is nothing wrong with this process as long as you are aware or conscious that you are no longer present in the moment. Instead, as you sit and plan, your focus shifts to an imaginary realm within your mind. What's important to distinguish is whether you are visiting the future through your spirit mind or objective mind. Plans made through the objective mind lack creativity and originality. These plans are usually connected to what you've seen or heard someone else do. They are usually very precise, detailed and aligned to specific dates. This type of planning is always met with the expectation that what we want to occur will *become* our reality in the distant future. However, planning can also be a form of daydreaming where you enter a sleeplike state and visit the future through your spirit mind. This type of planning comes from a creative space that is boundless and timeless, leaving room for what we want to occur at any given moment in any given shape or form.

The act of planning touches on our need to control and may signify that we are unsatisfied or discontent with the present moment. Thus, leaving the present for long periods of time can have a negative impact on our desired future. This is because we become attached to our thoughts and plans, causing us to overlook opportunities and events happening in the present moment. Any possible future outcomes are only accessible through the present moment. But the dreams that emerge from our spirit minds are connected to our destiny or as Paulo Coelho may call, our Personal Legend. But to know whether or not the future you desire is a part of your destiny, you must first understand and know how to connect to your spirit or "authentic "self", as mentioned in the first section of this book. If not, what you constantly desire and "dream" about may be nothing more than reflections of what others around you are thinking, doing and or dreaming. This is why it is important to remain aware and conscious within the eternal moment so that you can monitor what is entering your mind. Have you ever started singing a song out of nowhere and you thought to yourself, "Why am I singing that song, I must have heard it somewhere?" Sure enough, no sooner than you say this and become conscious of your actions, you notice the person a few feet away from you singing the song or a car in the distance playing the song. If you are not conscious of your surroundings and what the present moment may bring, you may mimic and carry out behaviors and various things happening around you all the time. Thus, who you think you are is merely a reflection of what surrounds you. As Buddha himself said, "Our life is shaped by our mind; we become what we think."

However, in addition to mental focus and awareness in the present moment, "feeling" is a key aspect to remaining in line with your destiny. Feeling involves using your intuitive capabilities and even your instincts that derive information from places that go beyond the scope and reach of your objective mind. But this means that you must be able to quiet your mind in order to tap into your feelings. If not, the feeling may only be a reflection or reaction to a thought produced in the mind versus an intuitive thought that is connected to a greater consciousness shared by the universe. Through feeling and responding to your "gut" response, you may access the supernatural and realms that your objective mind is unable to explain. Instead of thinking about the future, try moving into a space of "feeling" the present moment. Some people are able to "feel" what the future may bring whether we consider this to be a premonition, prophecy or foretelling. The vibrations that the body experiences, generated through pure "feeling", are almost equal to the feeling of the future experience itself. For instance, have you ever "felt" like you were about to win some money or that something good was about to happen. This feeling just came out of nowhere and wasn't directly connected to anything that you were specifically thinking or even doing in the moment. But the feeling was so strong that you almost felt like the money was in your hands at that very moment. There was no doubt in you whatsoever that this money was about to be yours and sure enough the money arrived not too far from that very moment. When you finally had the money in hand and you remembered the "feeling" you had, it gave you a great sensation and feeling of power that you were somehow connected to something greater working in the universe. But of course, this powerful force is always surrounding you and flowing through you and is accessible at any moment (and only through the moment).

When you think about the future, it may be difficult, if not impossible, to feel the present. And feeling the present will allow you to be able to visit the future.

Have you ever made vacation plans or planned out an event. You wanted everything to go exactly the way you envisioned because your plans were so perfect and beautiful. But as you began your trip or the event, something happened that didn't go according to *your plan*. Did you look at the occurrence as a sign or guidance from the universe or did you see it as a hindrance, problem or mistake? If your interpretation of what happened was that it was a hindrance then you probably began to curse the moment and even the universe (yes I've seen many people curse God). Chances are you went further into your mind and began to obsess on the "mishap", even though it had happened and was now apart of the past, because you couldn't seem to *let go* of your "plan". You couldn't let go of your thoughts of the past and your expectations of the future. At that moment you were disconnected from the flow of energy that the universe was directing you with (always for your greater benefit) and you actually began to move further away from experiencing something greater than what your objective mind could have imagined. As you probably sat complaining and groping about things not going accordingly or how you envisioned, *life was slipping right past you*. This may not happen all the time, but it definitely happens to people who leave no room for serendipity or for what the present moment may bring.

For some, they create a plan but they allow themselves room to change the plan in the moment and go with their "feeling" or as I like to say, "Go with the flow." For others, they use a minimal amount of planning to simply get them in route, but they set no expectations as they have already let go of selfish desires for a particular outcome. For these people, simply being, flowing in the moment and having the opportunity to experience life brings happiness. With an alert "feeling antenna", these people are also open to alternate routes to achieve their goals that may have otherwise been overlooked and disregarded because they did not exist in *their plans*.

Do you have your "feeling antenna" up and do you know how to use it? For countless centuries every ancient or pre-modern society has used some type of meditation practice to connect to their authentic self or the spirit world. Meditation involves focusing the mind. At the same time it involves going beyond the mind. For me, my meditation process works best during the morning when the atmosphere is very peaceful and I can only hear the sound of birds singing outside my window. Coming out of a deep sleep, my body is then more able to connect to the energy flow that is resonating around me. Thoughts beyond my mental plane begin to flow as I quiet my mind and simply "let go". I tend to pay particular attention to my breathing and the flow of air going in and out of me that brings my body life. Focusing on this present miracle enlivens my spirit and information from another realm may start to transfer through me. It has been through this process that I have been writing this book or how I figure out what I "feel" like wearing in the morning or how I figure out what I "feel" like doing some days when I don't have to work and how most of my creative products have been born and eventually materialized. Thus, silence and tranquility are key for me, but not totally necessary. Sometimes I am able to put my "feeling antenna" up while sitting in a crowded area with lots of commotion going on around me. In this scenario, I am still focused on "letting go" of what may physically surround me and through stillness of mind and even my body I can transcend undesirable thoughts and the physical world. But my favorite form of meditation aside from listening to the birds in the morning or even sitting near the ocean is simply being in the "act" of doing (a little chop wood and carry water). Whether it's an intense physical workout, making music, laughing with friends or strangers, cooking or dancing, these activities are meditative for me when I am able to lose my "mental self" in doing them and totally submerge my "spirit self" in them. In that eternal moment of activity, nothing else matters and nothing else exists as even time itself stops. At that point, I'm capable of losing even my thoughts about eating and sleeping. For countless hours I have stayed up making music or danced the night away only to be greeted by the morning sun outside. Have you ever taken a road trip with someone and had the most intense or incredible conversation and before you knew it you were suddenly at your destination? These moments represent various examples of being present and one with the moment because in them time stopped. When you can stop time, then you know that your "feeling antenna" is working, because to stop time you are exercising the power to "let go" of your egoic thoughts that are primarily concerned with the past and the future.

As I am getting more confident with my ability and power to let go of egoic thoughts, I have less need for plans and I've been able to find much more enjoyment, peace and liveliness through simply sitting calmly and allowing the future to come to me in the moment rather than seeking to envision and plan it. When I ask someone what they "feel" like doing, I don't expect for them to start thinking about an answer. I ask the question in hopes that they are able to connect to the present moment and their feelings. I am always willing to accept the answer offered and many times it's usually, "I don't know, what do *you* feel like doing?" When I'm not certain about what I feel like doing, I stick to my saying – "When in doubt, do nothing". For me, a lot of good may come from simply sitting still and being at peace with the moment instead *thinking* that I have to be doing something.

I have a friend in Los Angeles who is very intuitive and in touch with his "feeling antenna". For a while I stayed with him and his family and he taught me a lot about living in the moment. Every morning he would wake early and engage in his own form of meditation. During that process he would align himself with the energy flow. At a certain point in the day or the week he would allow him "self" (spirit) to indulge in whatever craving he was feeling. One time he drove many miles across town to get a slice of cake he was craving. From him, I learned the importance of not only listening and connecting to my spirit that communicates with my body through feeling but I also learned the importance of feeding (sometimes literally with cake) my spirit by living spontaneously in the eternal moment. The more I began to incorporate his outlook on life, the sharper my instincts and awareness became. I began to be able to distinguish between my mind/thoughts and my heart/feeling. I also began to be able to predict or foresee things and events. It's been several years now from the time when I lived with my friend and was learning from him how to trust my intuition, and currently, as I am writing this book, my confidence and faith in my "self" and my connection to the universe (all that exists) is incredibly strong. My fears are much less than ever before. I owe much to that experience and to my friend who did more living than planning. I realized that being self-employed is another key element to spiritual freedom and being able to let go. My friend did not have the same relationship with time, schedules or a routine like my friends who work for corporations or institutions that demand a great deal of their time. At the time when I was staying with my friend, I was unemployed so I was able to really experience the natural flow of things. I had just enough money to be able to satisfy some of my "feelings" for the most part and I can honestly say that that was a time in my life when I've been the most alive.

To Transcend Time (Let Go of the Past and Future)

"Yesterday is but today's memory, and tomorrow is today's dream."

- Khalil Gibran

Time is a construct of our rational, conscious mind. Time can be thought of as a "non-spatial continuum in which events occur". For some, time is a force that can be manipulated. Others believe that time is a dimension (The Fourth Dimension) that can be navigated. But what is most important to understand about time is that without memory, time does not exist. Every atom in the universe contains memory. This is how the universe is able to evolve as it builds on what it has already done or known. But there is a difference between the subconscious memory within atoms and the conscious memory within the human mind. In the spirit world, the past, present and future are all one. In fact, what we would consider to be seconds, minutes, days and years is all one eternal moment outside of our mental conception of time. For example, the Earth rotates on its axis and revolves around the Sun. This process is simply one continuous act. Nothing stops except our awakened state of consciousness once we go to sleep. It is due to the act of sleeping that humans may experience a sense of newness, a mental and physical recharge that seems to separate one wakened state from the next. However, what we may consider to be a "new" day, is nothing more than a fresher state of consciousness from past happenings/thoughts and a different position of the Earth in relation to the Sun. Our memory of those past happenings and thoughts are fragmented and this causes us to conceive the day as several individual moments. But in actuality life is one long event with naps and some forgotten stuff in between. However, our subconscious mind retains everything. If you want to experience what I mean, try staying awake and being active without sleeping for as long as you can.

As modern society continues to move further away from nature into a marriage with machine and computer technology, our way of life is becoming more and more defined by a "system of time". The modern human race, represented by "advanced" societies like the United States, is starting to act more like the machines and devices we consume. Did you ever wonder why cell phones and computers have clocks and are all in sync via satellite? Why do I need to have the "correct" time on my device that I use to talk to my friends or use to type a paper? I ask the question because I grew up in an era when even digital watches and clocks were not so popular yet and no one even had a computer. Telephones definitely didn't have clocks attached to them and it was common for someone to ask you, "Do you have the time?" But today we seem to be so attached to digital time that everything we do is time coordinated. We are more conscious of "time" today than ever before. In this sense, time consumes the average working person who is constantly on the computer or on the phone because it's right there staring at you! It makes total sense then that most people are always thinking about what they're going to be doing later, the tasks they have to complete, the errands they need to run, the paper they have to write or the conversation they had last week with someone, the great weekend they had two weeks ago, the birthday party that changed their life and the lists goes on and on and on. Actually focusing on the present moment for long periods of time without thinking about the past or the future begins to seem impossible.

You can't connect to the spirit world through the objective, intellectual conscious mind. For some, connecting to the spirit world is a scary thought because we've been raised in a society that is pretty much anti-spiritual and pro-secular. For instance, Yoga is a quintessential ancient spiritual tradition that somehow Americans have turned into a fitness program and fashion statement. In American mainstream films and television, spirits are portrayed as ghosts, belonging to a dark world and made to appear as something undesirable. Even catching the "holy ghost" in church is looked upon as something abnormal. This merely speaks to our ignorance of the spirit world and ways of life that place importance on spirit versus physical appearance. Being able to connect to the spirit world allows a person to experience a force of power that is undeniable. Through spiritual power we can accomplish miracles and things that the objective mind finds impossible to conceive or rationalize. Connecting to spirit allows a person to create things such as music, recipes, inventions, art, clothes and thoughts that are considered genius with the potential to impact the entire human race. Spirit is warm, beautiful, peaceful and harmonious. It is through connecting to the spirit of anything that we encounter, including our self, that we will find true and everlasting joy, happiness, peace and love. Love cannot be discovered or processed through our objective minds. Love is a force that cannot be understood intellectually. The truth is that the spirit, or all energy, is love and it can only be understood through feeling. This is why the spirit crosses over to its reverse self, the physical world, where "feeling" occurs, in order to experience itself – love.

If you've ever experienced true "love" with something or someone at any point, trust me, you were not thinking in that moment. If you can recall a "love moment" in your life, you will realize that your objective mind was inactive. You were in the moment or how I like to say, "in love". Because life is the moment and life is also love. Life resonates in the spirit. When we are truly focused on the moment and everything happening in that very instant, we are connecting to the very presence of life all around us and in us. This allows a person to fall in love with whatever may be a part of that moment. For instance, I remember the first time that I saw a DJ "cutting and scratching" records on two turntables in the early 1980's. I was hypnotized by his actions. The sounds and vibrations in the room produced a feeling that over came me. I wasn't standing there wondering when I'd start DJing or how I was going to get home or where he learned to do it. I just knew that I was enjoying the experience and after he finished, I knew that I wanted to be a DJ. In that moment, I had fallen in love with DJing and time had no impact on my love. Sometimes I will go years without touching my turntables and then out of nowhere I feel the urge to put some records on and start "cutting"!

If you want to experience love and life more often, I suggest that you start learning how to focus on the present moment by disconnecting from your thoughts. It's much easier when you are involved in doing something active like sports, cooking, drawing and the arts but you should be able to experience the moment anytime without having to be active. It's even hard for some people to stay in the moment while they're talking to someone. Most times people are simply dumping their thoughts about the past or future onto our laps. But this is when I'm most present in the moment to make sure that the mental toxins that a person is trying to release from their own incessant thinking doesn't seep into my subconscious and eventually affect my spirit. How can you learn how to be mindful or stay mentally present? It takes practice. Trust me, it takes a lot of practice to begin living our life in the moment because the majority of our life as adults has been lived on clock, calendar, past and future time. For me, I've been practicing the art of living in the moment consciously since about 2003 and I've just recently gotten comfortable with the new lifestyle. Living in the moment is definitely a lifestyle too, because much of living in the moment goes against the dominant societal norms that are most prevalent in urban cities. But I've been fortunate to find a group of friends and areas that embrace and/or allow for the "freeness" that living in the moment produces. Whatever you do, do not rely on drugs, alcohol, television and even some social activities to free your mind. What may start as a fun drink at happy hour can become addictive because of the "feeling" you're able to experience. Your life becomes a never-ending chase for that same "feeling" that you can only manufacture through drinking. Become the powerful spiritual being you inherently are and develop your ability to "feel" without the need of external things, people and/or activities. Begin by learning to sit for long periods of time by yourself in silence and focus on the millions of thoughts that keep popping in and out of your head. As you distance yourself from your thoughts, you will notice that there is another voice in your head talking alongside the thoughts telling them to stop. The whole experience can be quite bizarre. You will soon learn that the brain or objective mind never seems to stop, unless you consciously focus on something or until you develop the ability to turn it off. A great way to start is by learning to focus on something in the moment like your breathing or sounds (like birds singing). As you find yourself more in tune with the moment for longer periods throughout the day, you will be able to notice when your mind starts thinking thoughts that are disconnected from the present. That's when you can use that other voice to talk to your objective mind and say, "Hey just relax, let's think about that later. Right now is a good moment, let's enjoy it."

Living *Is* the Moment

"Letting go and detaching from outcome is the essence of genuine power and offers the only real possibility of security."

- Deepak Chopra

What does it actually mean to live in the moment? It means being mentally and spiritually present, aware and focused on right now. Yes, that means even while you're reading you should feel your "self" taking in these words and ideas. Feel your "self" breathing and looking at the page. Appreciate this moment, because it's happening. Remember that whatever thoughts you focus on, they may very well become your present reality at some point. Thinking continuously for extended periods of time inhibits our ability to appreciate the "now" in life.

I want to share a personal activity I do every so often to motivate my "self". Whenever I begin to feel a little burned out from my continuous work regime I take some quiet time with myself and imagine that I only have twenty-four hours left to live. It may sound a bit extreme but it works for me. I begin to ponder all the things that I'd do with the time I have left. Most times, simply the images of me fulfilling my wishes can bring me feelings of excitement, joy, gratitude and peace. I

begin to feel this way because as I'm daydreaming, I realize that I'm still alive and that I have the opportunity to fulfill my wishes. Somehow the thought of how temporary life is, wipes away my fears and hesitations. I imagine not having the opportunity to dance anymore, eat my favorite junk food, do my favorite things like people watch and lay on the beach, laugh with my friends and buy that pair of shoes I've always wanted. The thought of having a limited amount of time to live makes me say to myself, "Why not right now?" And usually the only thing stopping me is "me".

But it's impossible to truly live when you feel like you have something to lose. This is why to embrace life you must embrace death. Death represents transition and it is not final. Life and death are both endless processes. Each second of the day starting from birth marks another point between our arrival and our departure. A part of us constantly dies until our entire being eventually transforms. I think back as far as I can remember and recall aspects of my personality and body that are no longer a part of me now. I remember when I could eat anything that wanted without getting sick. Today, a piece of lettuce seems to add a pound. This is why it's important to embrace your current state of being and enjoy it to your fullest potential. I can recall so many times when I've passed up a really great pair of shoes or some clothing in the store because I was convinced that I couldn't afford it.

Once you realize that you have nothing to lose because you can never truly own anything (not even your own body), you will be able to approach the world with a carefree lightness. The first near death experience that truly put me on my path to realizing the beauty of embracing death happened during a road trip from Berkeley to Los Angeles, California. I was driving with my good friend Taryn and we ran into a hard rainstorm. I was driving at the time and out of nowhere the car started to hydroplane. I lost control of the car and we started spinning while crashing up against the side-rail. Although the car was totaled, Taryn and I walked away from the scene without a scratch. That next morning, feeling really shaken up from the accident, I walked to the corner food spot to treat myself to some fried fish. As I'm standing at the window to order my food a group of teenagers ride up on their bikes. One young man asks me for a dollar. Happy to be alive, I give it to him without hesitation. Within that same instance, a car had pulled up and it sounded like firecrackers going off. I immediately recognized that sound was an AK rifle and I could see the bullets ricocheting off the ground in front of me. Still in a daze from the car accident, I calmly pinned myself against the restaurant wall while the entire corner became instantly vacant. The entire incident lasted seconds. Strangely enough, I walked home feeling surprisingly serene and I began to cogitate on the symbolic relevance of the two events. What was the universe trying to teach or show me? The next day I made my decision to go back home to Brooklyn, New York to be with my childhood family. My money was almost all gone and I had no job waiting for me there. The move demanded complete faith. As well, I faced one of my greatest fears, flying, and I followed my heart to Brooklyn. Both the car accident and drive-by shooting allowed me to realize "here today, gone tomorrow." Within that quote, I now understand that I am unable to predict when, where or how my transition (death) will occur. Within both of those near death incidents, I can remember experiencing a strange beautiful feeling of peace that resonated throughout my entire being.

I had grown up as a child thinking that death was something to be feared and therefore it was bad. But now, with a deepened understanding and outlook on death, I regard death as one of the purest moments a being will experience. I do my best to think beyond the common thoughts of death as being merely a physical event. Death may also symbolize the transformation of thoughts that drain and stress you into thoughts that energize you. As you kill or cease negative thoughts, that space allows for pure consciousness to be born. Death may also symbolize simply letting go so that you may actualize death's opposite self – birth. Thus, expanding our outlook and relationship with death will interchangeably affect our relationship with time.

When fully submerged in the moment through pure consciousness (or focus on now), you will have the ability to become one with your surroundings and the universe. Through oneness, you will have the opportunity to communicate to loved-ones on the other side as well as with nature. Being tuned in to "now", will allow you to tap into the universal freeway of information.

JOURNAL EXERCISE:

Answer this question: If you found out that you had six months left to live, what would you do and how would you spend your time? Why are you not doing those things currently?

Forgiveness and Surrender

"You can not be lonely if you like the person you're alone with"

- Wayne Dyer

The power of letting go always allows us to both forgive and surrender simultaneously. When we let go of punishing thoughts, we are able to forgive others and ourselves. Forgiveness is one of the most powerful acts or states of being known to humans. Through forgiveness, we recognize that wrongdoing is not intentional. We allow our judgments and opinions of a moment to rest and allow the perfection of the universe to exist. Forgiveness is an ultimate act of love because when we forgive, we tap into an endless energy pool of love and gain internal understanding and wisdom that, what others do is never about us, it's about them. Even when we condemn ourselves for perceived wrongdoings or mistakes, it is merely our ego that is doing the finger pointing. But from our authentic self is where forgiveness will emerge. As the ego is never satisfied and is always focusing on its limitations or things that threaten its existence, our spirit possesses the power of pure love because that is the part of us that is infinite and all knowing. When you feel like you made a mistake, whether it's forgetting to do something you felt was important, saying something you wish you hadn't or that you could've said better or doing something you thought you could've done differently, the power of forgiveness supports the notion that everything happens for a greater reason and that our spirits are here to learn. What the ego considers to be a "mistake", the spirit knows is an opportunity to experience life and grow. When we interact with the world around us unforgivingly with eyes and thoughts of judgment, we stunt our spiritual growth. There is never a need to condemn and punish others nor one's self through judgment. Once you are able to forgive yourself, then it is easier to forgive others. Not being able to forgive says that things MUST be a certain way. When we try and control that which cannot be controlled, we set ourselves up to suffer frustration, anger, resentment, jealousy, disappointment and more.

When we lose "control" and let go, we not only forgive but we also surrender. We surrender the desires of the ego to always be right, safe and in command. Surrender allows things to simply be. There is no right or wrong. So what if you forgot to buy your boyfriend a birthday card. Surrender that thought and give power to the moment and share your love right now. A card doesn't equate love. However, your ability to let go of condemning thoughts that bring your energy level down is an act of love that will allow you to become present and share your "true-self" which is pure love (and better than any care I may add)! When you surrender, you allow yourself to be vulnerable and lower your guard or defenses. Many people fear vulnerability because it leaves them open to attack and pain, but that is merely fear itself speaking. The voice that tells us not to open ourselves to others is the ego talking, the place where fear resides. But just as a closed hand cannot give or receive, a closed or guarded heart cannot give or receive love. This does not mean that you conduct matters of the heart carelessly but instead you tap into your "inner self" that is intuitive and all knowing. And should someone turn out not to be who you felt they were, then simply forgive them and yourself and move on. Learning to listen to your heart takes practice. If it were easy to hear and follow the guidance of our perfect authentic self then our life journeys would be short and the evolution of the universe would be even shorter.

Practicing forgiveness and surrender allow us to experience all three states of being within the power of letting go. Through forgiveness, we let go of thoughts that do not serve to raise our vibration level in the moment. For instance, one day two friends and I were standing in line to eat at the school cafeteria when three people walked up and blatantly got in front of us. They didn't even acknowledge us. As the three of us looked at each other, I felt my body begin to tense, as I thought of things to say to the people cutting us in line. My heart rate began to speed and I no longer felt "good". I could see the anger building in my friend's eyes too. All of a sudden I said to my friends, hey let's just forgive them and surrender our spots in line. I went on to say that if they were that hungry then our compassionate selves should allow them to enter first because we were not suffering lose by allowing them to eat sooner. As my friends agreed, I noticed how our bodies loosened, our faces relaxed and our breathing slowed. We returned to a place of peace. Funny enough, just as we both forgave and surrendered, we realized that they were with the group of people in front of us. We laughed at ourselves and experienced the second state of being which is to let go of time. Once we let go of the need to eat sooner and found peace with the moment, we experienced true patience. Ironically, as our thoughts of anger and control diffused, the line seemed to move faster. It was then that I realized the final state of being – having faith. Because as I witnessed the miraculous power of forgiveness and surrendering our need to be in front of the people in line, a sense of love began to grow in my heart. I saw the people, who I once viewed as "out to get us and take our spot", as being no different than myself if I were meeting friends who already had a spot in line. My fear that I was losing something (whether it was getting into the cafeteria sooner, or that all the food would be gone or that people in line would think that I'm a push over) vanished. I chose actions in alignment with my god-self, placing my faith in love rather than fear.

When was the last time you forgave someone or yourself? How did it feel? Is there someone you hold in contempt and refuse to forgive? Surrender your fear and pain and allow forgiveness to free you.

Forgive at least five people or more, starting with your "self", everyday. If someone cuts you off on the freeway, instead of cursing them simply say, "I forgive you and I hope you make it to your destination safely and on time." Also, be sure to end each day with compassionate words to your "self" and forgive yourself for any perceived mistakes, hard feelings or any negative things you may have said to your "self" throughout the day.

Special Thank You (2001 – 2004)

Thank you Chayel for being my Master Teacher, you are one of the most patient and dedicated fathers that I know. Thank you Seanté for letting me stay with you all and for yelling at me to come inside when you found me sleeping in my car. Thank you to my cousin Bernie Billions for allowing me to live with you right when I needed it most; we've known each other since we were toddlers growing up in New York. Thank you little sister Rana for your unconditional love, you are the most giving and non-judgmental being I've ever met. Thank you Big Will for being my emotional anchor and stylist, you have the biggest heart on the planet. Thank you Troy for becoming the little brother I always wanted and for teaching me many valuable lessons on letting go. Thank you Jerome for telling me about that Nas video audition, that audition changed my life. Thank you to the Earle brothers (of Earle's Grill on Crenshaw) for supporting, teaching and feeding me. Thank you Karyn (of Café Buna) for being a beacon of light and for your example of excellence. Thank you Manu for being my lawyer and giving me motivation to keep going and introducing me to Dj Diamond. Thank you Tajai for being my musical partner and a true example of a "go-getter".

Thank you Defari for being my godbrother and a true rock star. Thank you to the Headbangers Crew (Yung Walt, Kryme, Q-Ball, Tonto, Automatic, Yung Dirty, Jimmy Godrocks, Southwood, Jamon and Classic) for trusting me and taking the musical journey with me; we had Crenshaw on lock for a couple of years! Thank you Q-Ball for being a leader and one of the flyest barbers that I know in Los Angeles. Thank you Dr. Scruggs for hooking me up with Inglewood Unified and for your influence that allowed me to start working even sooner. Thank you to everyone at Inglewood High School between 2001-2004 for being family to me (you all know who you are!). Thank you Lamarr for looking out for me and for your true friendship. Thank you A-Love for being an astute life learner, a connector and for always finding ways to involve me in projects. Thank you Kaveh B for being one of the best battle MCs I know and for showing me how to be fearless. Thank you Brandon for sleeping Hummer style so that we could keep our dignity. Thank you to Theresa and Ray for loving me, especially during a few visits back to the Bay when I had my hair in cornrows and my spirit was more hardened. Thank you Taryn for being so forgiving when I wrecked your almost brand new car driving through the Grapevine. Thank you Stacy Stace for being the first to call and tell me that

Aaliyah had passed. Thank you Norell for telling me to read The Alchemist!

Made in the USA
Columbia, SC
31 May 2023

17570416R00074